NAVAL HISTORY

AND

NATIONAL HISTORY

T0346186

CAMBRIDGE
UNIVERSITY PRESS

University Printing House, Cambridge CB2 8BS, United Kingdom

Cambridge University Press is part of the University of Cambridge.

It furthers the University's mission by disseminating knowledge in the pursuit of
education, learning and research at the highest international levels of excellence.

www.cambridge.org
Information on this title: www.cambridge.org/9781316626207

© Cambridge University Press 1919

First published 1919
First paperback edition 2016

A catalogue record for this publication is available from the British Library

ISBN 978-1-316-62620-7 Paperback

NAVAL HISTORY

AND

NATIONAL HISTORY

*The Inaugural Lecture delivered to the University
of Cambridge on Trafalgar Day* 1919

BY

J. HOLLAND ROSE, Litt.D.

(Hon. Litt.D. (Manchester); Fellow of Christ's College;
Vere Harmsworth Professor of Naval History in the
University of Cambridge)

CAMBRIDGE
AT THE UNIVERSITY PRESS
1919

NAVAL HISTORY AND
NATIONAL HISTORY

ONE of the chief tendencies of contemporary thought is towards specialization; and in no subject is this trend more marked than in history. As a result of the immense expansion of our knowledge of the past, and also of a laudable desire for thoroughness, historical studies have become divided into compartments, labelled ancient or modern, political or diplomatic, economic or social, ecclesiastical or archaeological, constitutional or legal, naval or military. Even these divisions are subdivided chronologically; and greatly daring is the student who ventures to delve deep into any one of these subjects for more than a century or two. This concentration of effort has manifest advantages as tending to promote accuracy and thoroughness; but it tends to become microscopic, and, if it be too meticulously pursued, produces narrowness of vision. A man who is perpetually engaged on a small portion of a subject loses the power of illustrating it from cognate studies; and the resulting limitation of outlook has prompted the remark of a cynic, that nothing in the world is so insufferably dull as a conversazione of specialists.

I have been led to these thoughts because the defects of over specializing have sometimes been conspicuous in naval histories, especially in those of a former age. Written generally with the purpose of describing a particular war or even a campaign, they attained their immediate object, but failed to achieve a wider success, that of arousing a general interest in their subject. If we ask why the earlier writers, and perhaps some of the later writers on naval history, failed to attract, the answer will be that they failed to connect their subject with the wider life of the age. As a rule they explained only briefly and perfunctorily why the war occurred, and they did not show how it stood in regard to previous conflicts, what principle was at stake, or how the course of world-history was affected.

6

The best instance of this limited out-look is the work of William James, "The Naval History of Great Britain," from the year 1793 to the Battle of Navarino in 1827. The six volumes of James's history offer a signal example of industry and perseverance. He consulted the logs of the ships which he named, and, when possible, interviewed their officers. Therefore the *Edinburgh Review* declared that his work "approaches as nearly to perfection in its own line, as any historical work ever did." This praise is deserved, if stress be laid on the words "in its own line." But readers of James soon become aware that that line was narrow. He follows almost exclusively the movements of fleets and ships. His volumes contain an enormous mass of details, generally very correctly and clearly set forth; but the details are united by no general plan. In short James gives us tactics without strategy, and he describes single engagements, while neglecting to take a survey of the war as a whole.

For example, at the commencement of his work, he traces briefly the growth of

the chief classes of ships of the Royal
Navy, and then plunges the reader into
the French Revolutionary War of 1793,
without presenting any account of its
cause except that the French beheaded
their king, whereupon we ordered the
French ambassador to leave these shores.
This neglect is the more singular because
the real cause of war was to some extent
naval; for the French were seriously
menacing the independence of our Ally,
the Dutch Republic, whose ports, ships
and money they meant to seize; and if they
established themselves in the estuaries of
the Scheldt and Rhine, they could threaten
the weakest side of the British Isles, the
long, exposed and easily accessible east
coast. A wider outlook would have enabled
James from the outset to invest his subject with general interest by revealing
the relation of the war of 1793–1801
to earlier conflicts; but that wider out-
look was not his. Instead of noting the
large issues of the time, James plunged
into details concerning the hostile fleets
and their movements at sea. This habit
of mind obsessed him throughout his

work, which, as the reader soon perceives, deals with the separate actions of British squadrons and single ships. It is not what it claims to be, a naval history; it is merely a history of the British navy.

The distinction between the two terms is important. The history of the British navy is, of course, the more restricted topic. It is concerned with the development of the fleet, both in *personnel* and *matériel*, its administration in peace time, its exploits in war time. It need not, I think, include the discussion of the wider aspects of strategy, for these depend largely on geography and national policy. The history of the British navy, as I understand the term, deals with the construction, administration and exploits of the fleet. The chronicles compiled with so admirable a care by James form, in my judgment, a perfect example of that limited but intensive treatment.

Naval history, however, ought to take a wider survey. It should comprise all the topics just enumerated, though it will deal lightly with the smaller details, such as single ship actions. But, while economising energy in regard to the lesser facts, it will launch out into wider realms; it will treat of economics, so far as that science influences the clash of interests at sea, the consequent growth of navies and the causes of maritime conflicts. Naval history will describe the chief geographical discoveries, especially the marine explorations of naval officers. To mention three cases in the period in question, Vancouver, Bass, and Flinders explored the coasts from California to Alaska, those of Victoria and Tasmania, and of South Australia—discoveries of high significance in the development of the British Empire. The naval historian will also show how the discoveries and settlements of the new lands induced new rivalries and influenced the policy of competing nations.

The clash of commercial customs and the growth of legal ideals will also come within the scope of naval history. To take two important episodes in the reign of George III; when the Armed Neutrality League was formed by Catharine II in 1780, the naval historian will not be content to say of her and the other armed neutrals that they were actuated merely by jealousy of England; or, as Captain Brenton says early in his "Naval History of Great Britain," the Dutch were induced by French intrigues to side against us. That explanation may satisfy a chronicler; it will not satisfy a naval historian. He will examine the complaints of the neutrals against British maritime customs as practised since "the rule of 1756"; and he will probably admit that at some points the neutrals had just cause of complaint against us. Similarly, when the League of the Armed Neutrals was revived by the Northern Powers in 1800 it will not be enough to state, as James does, that the renewed dispute turned on the case of the capture of the Danish frigate, *Freya*[1]. Conflicting theories of maritime law or custom, as well as personal matters, were at the bottom of the dispute.

Finally, to come to the present age, the student of naval history will be loath to shower on our recent policy

[1] James, *Naval History*, III. 41.

towards neutrals the epithets wherewith it has been plentifully bespattered, until all the evidence is forthcoming as to the motives which induced the Government to act very cautiously. For anyone who knows the history of the Armed Neutralities is aware how seriously they tilted the balance against us in the critical years 1780, 1801 ; also it is clear that in the still more critical years, 1915, 1916, the United States sympathized strongly with neutral claims, and, if we had trampled on those claims, might not improbably have adopted a distinctly hostile attitude.

Questions of this kind cannot be adequately treated without reference both to general history and to International Law ; and it may ultimately transpire that the tolerant conduct of the British Government towards neutral shipping was highly politic. Exasperating it was to those who were called on to deal with that shipping, which, doubtless, often adopted with impunity fraudulent devices ; but the caution of British policy, when contrasted with the reckless devilry of German submarine warfare, probably determined one of the larger issues of the war.

But there is another side to the subject of this lecture, viz. What is the attitude of the general historian towards naval history? On the whole, it has been unsatisfactory. Let us consider one or two instances. Macaulay will not be accused of prejudice against the senior service; for the very short account which he gives of its condition in the year 1685 is at least sympathetic. Yet in his brilliant introductory sketch of the making of the English people he scarcely mentions the influence of the Navy; and in his picturesque account of the reigns of James II and William III, the really excellent work of James II for the Navy is barely touched on, and the influence of sea power in deciding William's struggle with France and his re-conquest of Ireland is merely implied, and rarely, if ever, set forth. The only exceptions are his accounts of the Battles off Beachy Head and La Hogue; and these descriptions are vague, rhetorical and unconvincing. It is clear that the great historian regarded naval battles, still more naval policy, as outside his sphere, despite the fairly obvious fact that the fortunes of England were then decided by the Battle off Cape La Hogue, not by the showy conflicts at Steinkirk and Landen on which Macaulay lavished his pictorial power. Any careful student is well aware of the true facts of the case; yet, even now, they have not received due emphasis in the text-books.

Consider another instance. The volume in the "Political History of England" which deals with the reigns of Anne and the first two Georges is a careful piece of work; yet it is written almost entirely from the landsman's point of view. The friction with Spain in the New World is not clearly portrayed; and the trade disputes with her in the West Indies do not stand out as the fundamental cause of the war which began in 1739. Captain Jenkins's ear is duly presented to the reader; but the maritime and commercial issues then at stake are not explained. It is the same with the naval battles.

The two important successes gained in 1747 by Anson and Hawke over French squadrons are dashed off in fifteen lines, while the adventure of Prince Charles in 1745–46 occupies fifteen large closely printed pages. The thrilling events of that episode doubtless called for a full description; but, if so, why not describe a sea fight which at the outset nearly cut short the career of Charles? Setting out from St Nazaire early in July 1745, on board the armed sloop, *la Doutelle* (16), he was joined by a Dunkirker, the *Elizabeth* (64), but soon they were sighted and chased by H.M.S. *Lion* (58). Her captain, Piercy Brett, who had navigated the *Centurion* during Anson's voyage, made for the larger ship, closed with her at 5 p.m., and during five hours fought her at close quarters. At one time the *Doutelle* crept up astern of the *Lion* with the intention of pouring in a raking fire, but sheered off when pounded by the *Lion's* stern-chaser. Even so, the fight was unequal; but Brett and his men kept it up with dogged bravery until 10 p.m., when the *Elizabeth* was fain to sheer off towards Brest, leaving the *Lion* horribly mauled, with 45 killed and 107 wounded out of a total of 400. During the night the *Doutelle* stole away on her northerly course, and finally landed the prince and a few followers on the coast of Inverness-shire; but the magnificent exploit of the *Lion* crippled his expedition from the start by depriving it of the men and arms crowded on to the *Elizabeth*[1].

British sea power likewise cut off all French reinforcements for the Jacobites, and enabled the British Government to bring back from the Continent forces sufficient to ensure the overthrow of the Young Pretender.

Turn to the Seven Years' War. There the most dramatic incident is the capture of Quebec from the French; but in this triumph the share of Vice-Admiral Saunders and the fleet is generally omitted, and the exploit is hailed as due solely to a happy inspiration of General Wolfe and the valour of his troops. In point of

[1] See Appendix for Brett's modest account of his exploit, which is far too little known. Andrew Lang (*Hist. of Scotland*, IV. 452) notices it too briefly. He wrongly assigns 44 guns to the *Doutelle*.

fact, it was the activity of the ships and their flotilla of boats on the St Lawrence above Quebec which compelled Montcalm to spread out his forces widely, thus enabling Wolfe's inferior numbers to deal a telling blow just above Quebec, while a naval demonstration held a large portion of Montcalm's array on the Beauport cliffs below the city. All things considered, Saunders deserves as much credit as Wolfe for the final success of September 13, 1759. Yet one looks in vain in the *Encyclopaedia Britannica* for the name of Saunders.

Several other instances of neglect of the Navy by historians might be cited, did time permit. Too often (*e.g.* during the present war) they take for granted that British troops somehow reach a continental port and regularly receive supplies and reinforcements, the medium of transport being a kind of Arabian Nights' carpet, into the functions of which only a foolish inquisitiveness would venture to pry. Nine historians out of ten would probably sympathize with the remark of a very terrestrial humourist—

"the Navy is a huge mystery, hedged about by sea-sickness."

Even the influence of the Navy in furthering the expansion of the British race overseas has met with curiously slight recognition, though that influence availed, sometimes to found, always to shelter the infant settlements and to maintain their connection with the mother country in the times of their rich and tempting adolescence.

Moreover, in itself the growth of the Royal Navy is a fascinating theme, spreading over four and a quarter centuries. Its *continuous* life begins with the feeble efforts of Henry VII to build a Royal Navy, consisting of two ships, the *Regent* and the *Sovereign*; also with his foundation of Portsmouth dockyard in and after 1491 by the construction of a dry dock, on which with his habitual cautious thrift he spent the sum of £2061. 18s. 7d. British naval history tells of the great expansion of the fleet under the masterful impulses of Henry VIII, of its decline under Edward VI and Mary, of its splendid rejuvenescence under Elizabeth, its general neglect by the early Stuarts, its rise to world-influence under Cromwell, and thereafter of vicissitudes which made it more and more the barometer of national vitality and statesmanlike capacity. The Navy grew with our national growth, declined with our temporary decay, but recovered so soon as the life blood coursed freely in our veins and vision illumined the eyes of our leaders. And to-day the fleet is a greater power than ever, and that, not from ambition or greed of land beyond the seas, but from the imperious need of safeguarding our exports and imports, and of assuring free intercourse with the young commonwealths. Such a story is not a mere technical study reserved for experts; it tells of that which is part of our very life. The Navy is not a tool: it is not merely Britannia's trident, it is rather her right arm, extended seawards, feeble in her youth, still strong in her mature strength.

Contrast briefly the relations of the British navy to British national life with similar relations in the case of other peoples. The analogy with ancient Athens occurs to the mind ; for Athens trusted to her fleet and prospered only in the times of its efficiency. But, after all, she had but a brief existence as a great sea power. Only 75 years separated the first great triumph at Salamis from the disgraceful overthrow at Aegospotomi, after which the existence of the Athenian fleet was precarious.

In the modern world our first serious rival at sea was Spain. Yet, for all her maritime discoveries, Spain did not develop a Royal Navy until a few years before that risky venture, the Armada. Risky venture it was to cope with the trained crews and well adapted warships of the English navy. The islanders had 90 years of experience behind them ; the Spaniards, but very few years on regular ships of war of their own. In later times the Spanish navy had a creditable record, considering that that people was not by nature or inclination seafaring ; but since Trafalgar it has been of little account. Spain as a sea power can therefore claim not more than two and a quarter centuries of vigorous life. Rather less is the span of years of the Dutch navy, which began its wonderful career along with that of Spain, and after a gradual decline, virtually ended its days at Camperdown (1797). The French marine alone can challenge comparison with the British. Yet its continuous existence dates only from the time of Colbert's ascendancy, *i.e.* about 1680, or nearly two centuries after the birth of its northern rival. As for Prussia, it may be of interest to quote the remark of Captain Brenton, R.N. Writing his naval history in 1823, he said of her, "Prussia never could be considered a naval power[1]." Correct as a summary of the past, it was also a remarkable forecast of the future.

These salient facts as to the duration of the chief navies of the world have a special significance. In no other case has the national navy flourished during more than two and a quarter centuries. But the British navy, besides outstripping that span of life by two centuries, shows no sign of decline—not even of being

[1] Brenton, I. 21.

scrapped. Now, surely this means that the fleet is for us a more imperative necessity than it has been for any people. The necessity arose thus. As population increased, a larger and larger part of it had to live by exporting products to other lands, and by importing food from oversea. Consequently the industrial Britain of 1919 is far more dependent on the protection accorded by the fleet to its myriad maritime feelers than was the Britain of Nelson's age; and his age than that of Rooke; and his again than that of Drake. The need for a fleet in 1588 was in order to fend off the great army of Spain; now the need is not military, but economic, to guarantee the security of the new industrial England. It matters not what party is in power. Sooner or later (I pray it may be sooner) the pressure of this vital necessity will make itself felt; for, though the Navy, ever since the time of the early Tudors, has been an important factor in the national life, it was never so important as at present.

For these reasons I claim that in histories of the growth and spread of the English race the part played by the Navy has been far too much passed over. Even in great works dealing with the expansion of the English race the naval factor has been scarcely referred to, or has been summarily dismissed.

Not only writers but (what is far more serious) men of action are open to the charge of having almost ignored the Navy. Several British statesmen neglected the senior service, and that too, in times when maritime trade was rapidly increasing and called out for protection. Let us glance at the attitude of Walpole towards the Navy. No Minister had done so much to foster overseas trade as the thickset Norfolk squire. During the twenty years of his supremacy (1722–1742) commerce expanded by leaps and bounds. In the decade 1720–1730 imports and exports increased by 25 %; and no small part of that growth was due to the incursions of British traders into the close Spanish preserves of the New World. Sharp friction was the result, and one of the Spanish outrages is notorious. But there was more at issue than Captain Jenkins's ear. The real dispute was as follows—should Spain close the larger part of the New World to outside traders and submit "interlopers" to vexatious or barbarous treatment by her *Guardacostas*[1]? If she did, war was likely to result. Obviously, the last word in this long dispute was likely to rest with the British navy. Yet Walpole and his colleagues left the Navy practically stationary, and it could not act decisively until the latter half of nine years of war. Then, however, as we have seen it was the decisive factor. Thanks to the efforts of Anson and Hawke, the French marine was lessened by 12 sail, and great losses were inflicted on their mercantile marine. It is estimated that, in all, the French lost 664 merchantmen in the year 1747; and their plans in India and Canada were completely foiled. At home France felt the pinch so severely that her Controller of Finances declared in 1748 that, if hostilities continued, he

[1] See H. W. V. Temperley's article in *Transactions of the Royal Historical Society*, III. 200 *et seq.*

saw Hell open before him. Louis XV therefore made peace. True, his armies were victorious in the Low Countries and seemed about to overrun the territories of our DutchAllies. But the silent pressure of Britain's sea power compelled France to make peace.

What a singular peace it was from our point of view. "As you were" formed the *mot d'ordre* of the Treaty of Aix-la-Chapelle. In order to save Holland from conquest; in order to set up again the Flemish Barrier fortresses and place them in the reluctant hands of Maria Theresa, we sacrificed a great part of what the fleet had won. We gave back to the French the great naval stronghold, Louisburg, in Cape Breton Island, whence French men of war and privateers preyed upon the merchantmen of New York and Boston. Admiral Peter Warren, helped by the levies of New England, had captured that naval base, but now it was handed back, to the disgust of our Service and of the men of New England. It came to this, that the successes of the Navy more than counterbalanced the failures of the Army. Yet the political result was almost nil. Though the conflict had been from the start a maritime conflict, yet in the final treaty nothing was said about the Spanish right of search; and affairs were thrust back into the position which caused that conflict. Of course there soon resulted another struggle, the Seven Years' War. A further singular fact is that during the eight years of peace between the two wars, Parliament was persuaded to increase the Army, provided that the *personnel* of the Navy was cut down to 8000 men (1751).

Nelson said several times "We are a neglected service." But I question whether at any time the neglect of the Navy was more shameful than in that sordid age of Walpole and the Pelhams. The Navy saved the nation from ignominious defeat; yet the Government rewarded it with neglect at the peace and contumely after the peace. It is sometimes said that democrats and radicals have neglected the Navy. But it is impossible to find any case of neglect so

glaring as that just named, which occurred in the heyday of the supremacy
of the great county families.

By way of contrast to the downright
neglect of the Navy by Walpole and the
Pelhams, we may notice in passing the
enlightened resolve of the two Pitts,
father and son, to rely on it as the right
arm of Great Britain. During the in-
glorious war at which we have just
glanced, the Great Commoner vehe-
mently declaimed against the spiritless
defensive policy pursued at sea, "our
natural element"; and, when he came to
office in 1756, early in the Seven Years'
War, he adopted that vigorous offensive
at sea and wise defensive on the Continent, which pinned the French armies
to the Rhine and Weser, and wrested
from the *fleur de lys* Canada and India.

The part played by Pitt the Younger
on a far less promising *terrain* is much
less known, and deserves mention for its
statesmanlike foresight. Never was England at so low an ebb as in the year 1783,
when he became Prime Minister at the
age of 24. Then, at the end of that

disastrous War of American Independence, he found the nation nearly bankrupt and sharply divided. The Navy also was divided; for under the administration of the Earl of Sandwich (1771–1782) it became the tool of the Tory party, Sandwich using it openly for purposes of partisan jobbery. The wonder is that Rodney and Hood won their brilliant successes in 1780–2; for Admiral Sir T. Byam Martin asserts that, on the fleet being paid off at the disastrous peace of 1783, not a single ship was found to be sound; several had foundered on their homeward voyage.

Such was the state of things confronting the young Prime Minister. Undauntedly he faced it. Though bankruptcy was imminent, he saw that money must be found for the fleet. Parsimonious elsewhere, he was liberal to it. Byam Martin testifies to "his protecting vigilance in watching over the colonial, maritime and commercial interests of the country." He used (says Martin) "to visit the Navy Office to discuss naval matters with the Comptroller, and to

see the returns made from the yards of
the progress in building and repairing
the ships of the line: he also desired to
have a periodical statement from the
Comptroller of the state of the fleet,
wisely holding that officer responsible
personally to him, without any regard
to the Board[1]." The Comptroller then
was Sir Charles Middleton (afterwards
Lord Barham), who ably held that important office during the years 1778–90.
Middleton states: "Such was Mr Pitt's
liberality in the grants that by the time
I quitted the Board we had upwards of
90 sail of the line fit for service, and
all their stores ready for putting on
board[2]." Think of it: 90 sail of the
line ready for sea in 1790, as against the
Rotten Row of 1783. That is what
made Spain in 1790 give way during the
Nootka Sound dispute about the lands
now called Vancouver Island and British
Columbia. That, also, is what made
H.M.'s Navy ready for the next war
with France, signalized by the exploits

[1] *Journals and Letters of Sir T. Byam Martin* (N. R. S.),
III. 379–381.   [2] *The Barham Papers* (N.R.S.), III. 30.

of Howe and Hood, Jervis and Duncan, Nelson and Collingwood. Those exploits would have been impossible but for the enlightened patriotism of Pitt in using every pound possible for the Navy and expediting the work of the dockyards; for it is at the Admiralty, the dockyards and in the training ships that the war of the future is won or lost.

The work of the two Pitts for the Navy marks them out as the fathers of that service in their times. They saw what the fleet meant to England and they resolved that she should be supreme at sea. Yet so soon as their invigorating influence ceased, the relapse into torpor or inefficiency was sudden and startling. In truth, there was in this land no well established school of naval thought. The professional experience of my Lords of the Admiralty somehow did not permeate the Cabinet; and it is not easy to explain why the Admiralty had so little weight in the councils of the nation. Consider this curious fact. After Pitt the Younger retired from office in 1801, his place was taken by Addington, one of the weakest of British Prime Ministers; yet, though he had by him one of the strongest First Lords of the Admiralty that we ever had, the Earl of St Vincent ("old Jervie"), it was not St Vincent's strength but rather Addington's weakness which determined the conditions of the Treaty of Amiens (1802). Wretchedly weak they were nearly all round, but especially in regard to naval policy. Let me explain matters briefly. By the conditions of the Treaty of Amiens Great Britain virtually retired from the Mediterranean. She pledged herself to withdraw her troops from Egypt, to give back Malta to the moribund Order of the Knights of St John, and she also restored Minorca to Spain. Thus the British fleet was to be left without a single sure base east of Gibraltar.

Now, this withdrawal from the Mediterranean was in defiance of all past experience, even of the very recent experience of the years 1796–8. In 1796 we had been fain to evacuate that sea because Spain had lately joined France against us; and at the end of that year

Jervis and Nelson sailed out, with rage in their hearts at this craven policy[1]. What was the result? In the next year Bonaparte set on foot designs for the conquest of the whole of Italy, the seizure of Malta, and the conquest of the East. Speedily we had to send in a fleet under Nelson, whose triumph at the Nile led to the recovery of our shattered prestige, and the eventual capture of Minorca and Malta. Events had proved, therefore, that when the Union Jack retreated from the Mediterranean, that sea tended to become a French lake, opening up the portals of the golden east to our then persistent enemy. Yet at the Peace of Amiens naval considerations were so far ignored that the blunder of 1796 was once again perpetrated. Those keys of the Orient, Malta, Corfu, Egypt, were left almost defenceless, and therefore an irresistible temptation to the restless ambition of the First Consul of France. As for the victory of the Nile and the capture of Minorca and Malta by Duck-

[1] Nicolas, *Dispatches of Nelson*, ii. 290; *Spencer Papers*, (N. R. S.), i. 319.

worth and Keith, those successes might never have happened, and the larger issues of the years 1796—1800 might never have been set forth as beacon lights for the future. The blood of our seamen seemed to have been shed for nought; and all because the ship of State was at that time steered by those who had no eye for the teachings of naval history. The divorce of naval affairs from national affairs was complete; and therefore Trafalgar had to be fought in order to settle again questions which, with average wisdom and firmness, might have been settled at the Peace of Amiens.

Do not misunderstand me. I am not claiming that every place which British seamen capture should remain British at the ensuing peace; for, if so, half the world would now be coloured red. No: moderation in victory is one of the highest of political qualities, and it leads to an assured peace. But my argument against the Treaty of Amiens, as earlier against that of Aix-la-Chapelle, was that those compacts were unintelligent, and therefore did not make for an assured peace. They ignored the teachings of history and the promptings of experience. Take another instance of harm resulting from the lack of acquaintance with the lessons of naval history. This case belongs to a period which was fondly supposed to be one of universal and lasting peace— I mean that of the beginnings of the Crimean War. It is in a time throbbing with generous impulses and vague enthusiasms that the lessons of experience are most apt to be scouted; but when they are scouted, harm soon follows. So it was in 1854. The nation was very ill prepared for war, and so was the Aberdeen Administration. *Ex uno disce omnia.* War having been declared against Russia on March 29, Instructions were drawn up for Vice-Admiral Dundas, commanding the British Fleet in the Black Sea. They were drawn up, not by the Admiralty, but by the Duke of Newcastle, who was at that time both Minister at War and Minister for the Colonies, and was not inappropriately described as the Minister at War with the Colonies. He drew up the Instructions, and (so far as the official records show) they were sent out with no official comment whatever by the First Lord of the Admiralty, Sir James Graham. Let us transfer this incident to the early days of August 1914, and try to imagine Lord Kitchener drawing up the Instructions for the Grand Fleet over the head of Mr Winston Churchill, and the latter forwarding them without a murmur to Admiral Jellicoe. Imagination droops at the thought of it; and our ears tingle at the mere suggestion of the rich sea vocabulary that would flow forth against the Junior Service for daring to dictate to the Senior.

If I had time I could point out some of the defects in the Duke of Newcastle's Instructions; but the fact that His Grace ever wrote them at all is the enormity; and we should have liked Sir James Graham better if he had substituted his own.

This, then, is another instance of disregard of naval experience. If the War Office had then consulted the Admiralty and regarded the Black Sea campaign as an amphibious expedition, far more effective plans might have been devised against the Russian army which had crossed the Danube; and if they had been crowned with success, the subsequent expedition to the Crimea might have proved to be unnecessary.

Hitherto my lecture has been of an ultramarine tinge. I have been indulging in criticisms of civilian officials such as will rejoice the hearts of naval officers, who in general find a new zest in life when they fall foul of "the politicians." But let me say that, though history frequently has to set forth the shortcomings and misdeeds of politicians, yet it must (if it is fair) show that sometimes they have been accused unjustly by the men in blue. The fact is that the point of view of the naval officer and of the ordinary civilian Minister is very different. The one thinks mainly (perhaps solely) of the fighting efficiency of the Navy: the other has to think about taxation; he has to face the complex yet imperious needs of a growing community which demands reforms here, reforms there, which calls out for a higher standard of living and a lower standard of taxation. There is the rub. The modern man wants a very great deal, yet he objects to paying a very great deal for it. Now, here we touch on the chief difficulty of a British Administration. Any thinking and fair minded man can see the difficulty now ; for it is appalling. But to a lesser degree that difficulty has always confronted British Ministers. They had to do with a people essentially the same as ours in temperament, rather shortsighted as to coming perils, but keenly alive to present discomforts ; therefore inclined to resent heavy taxation for the navy and army, and likely to overturn an Administration which sought to impose it. Moreover, we must remember that the England of the eighteenth century (to go no further back) was a poor little country, and literally could not afford to keep up a big navy, still less an army, on a war footing. Political prejudice absolutely forbade an attempt in the case of the army ; and it was not wholly inoperative against a large standing navy. Consequently, England partly from poverty, partly from prejudice, was always unprepared for war; and this, not so much from the fault of Ministers, as from the crotchety notions of the people. Rather than bear the perpetual strain of complete preparedness for war, they put up with the brutality of Press Gang methods when war did come. The fact that the English folk, even from Anglo-Saxon times, used to impress men for the navy, when there was need of men; and the fact that the Press Gang was used brutally and remorselessly and was not abolished by Act of Parliament until 1833, show that we were content to jog along, meeting each crisis when it came, *not* preparing for it systematically.

Naval history, then, will take into account the shortcomings of the nation at any given time before it blames the Government then in power. It will also try to gauge the difficulties of Ministers in finding out in a time of dispute what our opponents are likely to do. Probably it is well within the limits of truth to state that, for one dispute that ends in war, there are three disputes that blow over without war. After spending many years in the study of war and diplomacy I cannot help expressing my deep sympathy with statesmen who try to avert a rupture and think they have averted it; yet find the horror upon them. Worst of all, they are often blamed for not having forewarned and forearmed the nation.

The problem of judging the probabilities of peace or war is more complex, more vitally important, than ever; and it will tax the best brains of Britain to solve it. They will have to gauge the national forces of to-day and note whether they are tending towards a peaceful League of Nations or another world-war. They will frame friendly agreements or alliances, yet without pinning their faith to them for a long term of years. Above all, they will make it clear to all Powers, that Great Britain cannot forego her great marine insurance, the Navy, unless the new *régime* of international brotherhood and peace shows signs of enduring stability.

In view of these dubious developments the difficulty of assessing the future is greater than ever. Can history throw any light on it? I think it can. As in Biology the investigator often learns about the mature organ by studying it in embryo; so too the naval problem of to-day may be illuminated by throwing on it the searchlights of the simpler past. At any rate in our studies of the beginnings of wars, we shall, I think, come to see the very real difficulties of statesmen in foreseeing the course of events. Doubtless, in some cases they were grievously at fault, and suddenly threw on the two services a very unfair burden of responsibility. In other cases hostilities began so unexpectedly as to set at defiance the reasoned forecasts of statesmen. Each case must be judged on its own merits; and the student of war never deals with a more important topic than when he seeks to discover what are those merits. On this question naval history, if it is in close touch with political and diplomatic history, can hold an even balance in the eternal feud between naval officers and "the politicians." Perhaps the consideration of past problems of war and peace may do something towards establishing a better understanding between those opposites.

To sum up then. There ought to be a close connection between naval history and national history. To separate the two is to make of the former merely a jejune technical study; to set forth the life experiences of the English folk without adequate reference to the naval factor is like describing the life of a duck apart from water. The work of correlating naval and national history is, of course, no new development. It has been undertaken with conspicuous success by the late Admiral Mahan of the United States Navy and by Sir Julian Corbett, of Trinity College, Cambridge; and it is only fitting that we should remember that the foundations of modern naval history were laid broad and deep by the late Sir John Laughton, Honorary Fellow of Gonville and Caius College, Cambridge. It is for us to try to add something to their work; and by so doing we shall open out new vistas into the rich and varied life of the British people. The subject ought to attract students; for it offers a field of research that is less worked than political, diplomatic or economic history; and at several points it opens up fascinating glimpses of effort and achievement, often by little known officers.

May I close with a personal reference? At the time when the late Professor Gwatkin was appointed to the Dixie Professorship of Ecclesiastical History, I had the privilege of speaking with him, and he told me that it would be his chief endeavour to bring that special subject always into close relation to the main current of national life, not to handle it as something apart from general history. I believe that I cannot do better than indicate my ideal in terms analogous to those employed by Professor Gwatkin. How well he succeeded in the carrying out of his ideal is known to all sons of Cambridge. My execution of a not wholly dissimilar duty will be far inferior to his; but at least I can claim that my ideal is similar. While not neglecting the details of marine warfare (for indeed these furnish the basis of the whole subject), I shall try to set forth fully the reasons why maritime wars broke out, to explain and criticize the main lines of naval strategy, adopted on either side, to show how far Sea Power determined the issue of the struggle and to inquire whether the ensuing peace corresponded to the conditions of the time. In short, my aim will be to teach, not merely the annals of the British navy, but also naval history in its widest sense.

APPENDIX

THE FIGHT OF THE *LION* AND THE *ELIZABETH* (July 9, 1745)

Capt. Brett to Thomas Corbett. H.M.S. Lyon, *Plymouth Sound,* 19 *July,* 1745.

(Admiralty, In Letters 1/1481)

I beg you'll please to acquaint the Rt Hon. Lords Commissioners of the Admiralty that on Tuesday the 9th inst. being in the Latitude of 47. 57 N. and W. of the meridian of the Lizard 39 leagues I saw two sail to leeward of me standing to the Westward close upon a wind. The wind was at NNW. I accordingly bore down to them and by 3 in the afternoon I plainly saw they were two of the enemy's ships. By four o'clock I was within two miles of them; they then hoisted French colours and shortened sail. One was a man of war of 64 guns and the other a small ship of 16 guns. At 5 I run alongside the man of war within pistol shot and begun to engage. By six my mizon topmast was shot away and soon after that my mizonmast and mizon yard came down upon deck. By 8 o'clock the quarter of my mainyard and fore-topsail yardarm was shot away and main topsail yard in the slings. By 9 all my lower masts and topmasts were shot through in many places, both main stays, all the main shrouds but two, one on the larboard side and one on the starboard, the Braces, Bowlines, Topsail Halliards, Jeers, Lifts, Tacks & Sheets all shot to pieces, so that I lay muzled and could do nothing with my sails. The ennemy did not receive much damage in his masts & yards, but his Hull must have suffered greatly. At ten o'clock he sheered off and as he was going I gave him a farewell with two of my four & twenty pounders; but he made no return and in less than an hour was out of sight, and my condition was such I could not follow him. The small ship in the beginning of the Engagement made two attempts to Rake me, but I soon beat him off with my stern chase. He did us little or no harm, and after that lay off at a great distance.

From the beginning to the end of the Engagement we kept a continual fire at each other about the distance of pistol shot. The *Lyon's* hull is very much shattered as well as her masts, yards & rigging, two of my guns dismounted and the Palm of my best Bower anchor shot away, 45 of my men killed and 107 wounded; 7 have died of their wounds since the Engagement.

The next morning at daylight I saw the Enemy to the Southward of me making the best of his way to some Port in the Bay of Biscay, and as the small ship was not then in company, I imagine he proceeded on his voyage to the Westward. It was near 24 hours after the engagement before I was in a tollerable condition of making sail. Both my spare topmasts and yards were shot through in five or six places so that I had not one mast or yard to make use of in the room of those which were wounded and shot to pieces.

As my greatest Dependence during the Action lay in the alertness of my officers in their severall stations I should be ungrateful if I did not beg leave to acquaint their lordships that they all behaved extreamly well except the Captain of marines....My master lost his

45

right arm in the beginning of the engagement, my lieutenants were all wounded two hours before it was over, but notwithstanding that, encouraged the men at the guns to the last. My first Lieutenant was so much hurt that he was obliged to be carried off by 9 o'clock, not being able to stand any longer. The Ennemy seemed to be full of men and I dare say had many Expert gunners, for he seemed to place his shot wherever he had a Mind. His lower teir were Brass, of 24 pounders, his upper teir of 12 pounders and those on the Quarter Deck & Fore Castle, 6 or 8 pounders. As I was not so happy as to take him, I have only this satisfaction left that I spoiled his voyage. But if my behaviour should meet with their lordships approbation I shall think myself very Happy and am etc.

www.ingramcontent.com/pod-product-compliance
Ingram Content Group UK Ltd.
Pitfield, Milton Keynes, MK11 3LW, UK
UKHW042141280225
455719UK00001B/7